SUPERNATURAL LEADERSHIP

CARLOS XAVIER CHAVEZ

SUPERNATURAL LEADERSHIP

Scripture quotations marked NLT are taken from the Holy Bible, New Living Translation, copyright © 1996, 2004, 2007. Used by permission of Tyndale House Publishers, Inc. Carol Stream, Illinois 60188. All rights reserved. Website

Scripture quotations marked NKJV are taken from the New King James Version. Copyright © 1982 by Thomas Nelson, Inc. Used by permission. All rights reserved.

Scripture quotations marked KJV are taken from the King James Version of the Bible.

iUniverse books may be ordered through booksellers or by contacting:

iUniverse
1663 Liberty Drive
Bloomington, IN 47403
www.iuniverse.com
844-349-9409

facebook.com/CarlosX.Chavez
9094520952
pastorcarlosX@yahoo.com

ISBN: 978-1-6632-0555-1 (sc)
ISBN: 978-1-6632-0556-8 (e)

Print information available on the last page.

iUniverse rev. date: 08/11/2020

INTRODUCTION

Leadership is my passion and it has become lifestyle. I have dedicated over twenty years of my life in leadership, and have imparted in others what God has given me. I have inspired all types of people to rise up and do something in life. My intention is to make the difference in loving God, sharing that love of God, and loving my neighbor how God has commanded. I just want to be a vessel in the hands of the Lord and say to you that being happy is not difficult. Let me share something with you, I would rather be practical and communicate something from God, then to be eloquent and confuse you and lead you into error. I will make it simple, and fun, just how I am, a young pastor that rejoices in life and believes in the calling that God has given him. Dear reader, with just a few words, that is my intention.

This is why God has permitted me to present you this book, for the edification of the children of God. To take them to another level in their lives as christians, as parents, sons, brothers, as entrepreneurs, or in any area where you need to make a decision to undertake leadership.

At this moment in life, exists a great necessity in this world, I am speaking of the great need for model leaders. Model leaders that our generation is willing to follow or be inspired by them, so that the potential of every individual may be projected until achieving the purpose of why God has brought us into this world for.

Something that has caught my attention in studying the bible; I have realized that nothing that occurs in this world occurs without a persons determined capacity. God himself has placed that determination within human beings, and nothing may intervene in the matter. Wow! God moves in favor of his leaders here on earth. We are guilty for what occurs or never occurs.

We have seen mans leadership from Adam and Eve, Cain and Abel, Noah, the patriarchs: Abraham, Isaac, Jacob, the judges, Deborah, the Prophet Samuel, King David, etc. But, when we look at the most followed leader in the history of humanity, his name is Jesus, His life became a great example and inspiration for leadership.

Jesus never jumped the authority of John, which God himself had given him. Jesus is baptized after approximately thirty years of process. Jesus undertakes his voyage to the desert where he receives the most difficult test for a leader, to be tried by the temptations of success, obstacles, pains, sleepless nights, efforts, etc. But, he took the path of process. He understood that success is not obtained in one day, but daily, until obtaining it. Later, Jesus forms a working team, in which Jesus will reproduce his leadership in them. As a mentor and a spiritual father to them. Jesus left us a great example, that every supernatural leader needs a working team that will leave a legacy from generation to generation until eternity.

With this book I want to inspire you to achieve what I have called Supernatural Leadership. You will not be but inspired by the power of the word of God which is supernatural. This book will impulse your life to attain goals and achievements that will help you reach success.

We all know the importance of leadership, but it is more than that, the importance of someone arising as a leader, making the difference in all places, moved by the will of God. it is about taking leadership to influence a group of people to revolutionize and transform a company, ministry, or church. The supernatural leader is like a Captain who navigates people through the ocean of life, which requires for that leader to see what others do not see to plan the destiny of the voyage, and to discern the dangers of the path. The leaders goal is to lead the boat to its destination of growth, production, and success.

Someone once said that the church is like a boat that navigates through the ocean and we must take it to its destination. But the problem is that there are many churches that have already been established, but they are like a boat in the dock or port, these boats have never been able to sail to deep waters because of the lack of a leader to inspire them to navigate and get out of the comforts and security of the port. A great leader is always aware of the dangers of navigation, but is conscience that a boat was built to navigate through the ocean. Just like the church was built to go out and work for the kingdom of God and win souls. Taking on new routes and challenges that lead us to the ends of the earth to preach the good news. Not only is a boat navigated, but the boat must also take people to their destination. In the same way, the church must retain the souls, and equip them forming a team within itself, training others until each person reaches their destiny for which God has called them, and achieving multiplication, expansion, and success.

This book will help you perfect your level of authority as a leader, through means of biblical principles. molding our character to be able to acquire a level of grace and favor with other people, without violating the principles that have already been established by God. Many known pastors, friends, and business owners have been able to obtain higher levels of leadership thanks to the advice God has allowed me to share with them. In this book I will give you the secret so that people will want to follow you and long to be closer to you. For you to achieve those super natural things that no eye has seen and no heart of man has discovered. To achieve them, you must form a working team that can follow you to fulfill the dream of God designed for you.

With tears of love I write this introduction, hoping for the Holy Spirit to touch your heart. And help you understand the importance of establishing leadership in every congregation, in such a way that we equip every disciple, so each one of them, may achieve being better in every area of their lives and be a true examples for the generations to come. I pray for our pastors, our ministers, levites, and disciples from all the congregations, so that you receive the principle vision that our supernatural leader Jesus Christ entrusted us, saying, "Go therefore and make disciples of all the nations, baptizing them in the name of the Father and of the Son and of the Holy Spirit, teaching them to observe all things that I have commanded you; I am with you always, even to the end of the age." Prepare yourself and we will begin in the name of Jesus Christ. God will make of you a supernatural leader.

CHAPTER 1

THE DEFINITION OF LEADERSHIP

Leadership is the set of directive abilities an individual has to influence in peoples way of being or in a group of determined people, making sure that this team works with enthusiasm to achieve goals and objectives.

It is also understood like the ability to take initiative, gesture, seek, promote, motivate, give incentive, and evaluate a group or team.In business administration the leadership is the exercise of executive activity in a project, in an edifying and efficient way, wether this be personnel management, or institutional.(within the administrative process in an organization). Author Richard L. Daft, in his book (The experience of leadership)defines leadership as the influences of relations that occur within the leaders and their followers, by means of which both parts pretend to come in terms to changes and results that will reflect the purpose they share.The basic elements of this definition are; leader, influence, intention, responsibility, change, shared purpose and followers.

The original sense of the word "leading", comes from the word "lead" that became a common word to all the ancient tongues of northern Europe such as (Holland,German Anglo-Saxon, Norway,Danish,Swedish),and it means path, route, course of a ship at sea, and Journey. meaning that it remains rarely unaltered in these languages .A leader accompanies people on a journey, guiding them to a destination.This mean keeping them united like a group while he conducts them in the right direction.However the term "leadership" has been defined from different approaches;

Leadership is the process of being an influence, guide, or directing the members of the group towards consequence of organizational objectives and goals.

Leadership is having the ability to decide what needs to be done,and then achieve for others to want to do it.

Effective leadership is the one that produces movements towards the interest of the group for the long term.(Kotter, 1990)

"Directors do things correctly, but leaders do the right things"(Bennis,and Nanus).

A leader is a person that has the ability to create influence on others,to lead them, and guide them effectively towards achieving their organizational objectives and goals.

A leaders most important role is to influence in others to achieve with enthusiasm the objectives suggested.(Mintzberg,1980).

Definition and description of a supernatural leader:

A supernatural leader can be described as a person with the ability to inspire others, influence others, achieving for individuals or multitudes to voluntarily follow him, until they reach a point of reproducing a vision and a specific purpose.Always identifying and developing the gifts and talents of those that follow him.Leaving in the follower a legacy and an eternal purpose, taking everything that God has promised him and taking it without doubting in the power God has granted upon birth, and operating in new dimensions both spiritual and physical. Establishing principles and eternal values, always checking what Gods perfect and pleasing will is.Demolishing fortresses and obstacles, taking decisions, not because of circumstances, not because of feelings, but because of convictions. Always waiting for constant success and progressive in what has been planned. Faith is your automotive and love is your motor and your actions are your best support.

The supernatural leader is a server, every time he sees a need it's an opportunity for the supernatural to manifest. He supply's what is missing, he makes a difference, defeats evil with good, and he can discern what others can't see.If he has to ask for help then he will do so because he has that virtue to recognize his limitations. Although he depends on God, and knows that God manifest in his creation.That makes him a wise and prudent man, because God is the fountain of blessings and will always be conscious of the spiritual and material world, knowing that the more he knows God, the more he will know his creation.

CHAPTER 2

ENEMIES OF LEADERSHIP

1. **The largest enemy**, to rise up and oppose you to not undertake this new phase in your life is right in front of this book, It is you.

It is sad to see in many churches, ministries, families, businesses, teams, etc., that a lot of people oppose creativity, innovation, progress, or any other effort to lead to excellence and success, with the excuse that what they have been doing has worked. It is necessary to know that just because it has worked until this day it doesn't mean it's the best thing, or the peak, or the highest production.

Friend, that is reading this book, our supreme leader experienced this same opposition; Jesus Christ being criticized, persecuted, and questioned for bringing to this world the solution to sin, the new pact of grace. I am sure that you will also experience the opposition to growth in all aspects of your life, from ministry to business ventures. I, myself, in the process of life, experienced this opposition, discovering that my worst enemy was my mentality of old wine, but thank God for the new wine, he poured out on me,his Holy Spirit, which took care of renewing my mind.

Dear reader, this is the best moment to ask the Holy Spirit through a prayer that he be the the fountain of knowledge and bring conviction to your mind and heart. Ask him to show you all the areas that you need to give up and surrender so that they may never interfere with your material and spiritual growth, That is the key to a supernatural leader. As you go through the pages of this book you will be conquering yourself, and seeing your old self, along with the mental strongholds being conquered, and you will see a supernatural leader be born, the one that was hiding inside of you.

I hope that you made this prayer because this book is about supernatural leadership, which will go beyond tangible or visible. This is where I want to transmit one of the main objectives of this book, it is to achieve inspiring a new generation, conscient that every human being is composed of spirit, soul, and body, and if we ignore one of these areas soon we will find ourselves in problems. If you ask yourself why? The answer is noticeable with much fear of God, and with a passion to want to contribute something to repair the walls of our generation, metaphorically speaking, lacking repairs, like the walls of Jerusalem in the times of Nehemiah.

There are many prosperous ministries that are very used by God, there are families, businesses, etc., that believe that because they are having success or prosperity, they neglect their spiritual side or their soul. You could be good physically, but sooner or later there will be a manifestation of the fruits that you have sown, and all seed takes time to give its growth, the same concept applies for the good as for the bad. I'll explain it to you through this example. If Eve would of came to Adam with the consequences manifested of her disobedience, Adam would have never tasted the prohibited fruit, but like forgetful beings, we never remember that everything that we plant some day we will reap, and all harvest takes its time.

Without further preamble.

My desire is to awaken this truth, just like faith and works are married, the reap and the harvest, worship and service, also, leadership and supernatural leadership should be linked.

Every person that undertakes a leadership, can not let their guard down and be practicing impure things, it is sad to see the quantity of ministers that watch pornography or practice lust, or steal from his neighbor, love money, or business men that because they have their family with all material things, think they can do whatever they want, violating the laws, adulterating and abandoning their homes. Believe it or not, every human being that neglects an area whether it is spiritual or material, will have consequences. Read: 1 Thessalonians 5:23

"Now may the God of peace himself sanctify you completely; and may your

whole spirit, soul, and be body be preserved blameless at the coming of our Lord Jesus Christ." 1 Thessalonians 5:23 (NIV)

Now i ask you, "Can this be possible to evade and do what is right?" I always say, if you can dream it, it can be a reality. If you believe it, it can be possible. And if you embrace it today, you will obtain it. Now, lets touch another point of the word leader.

Dear Christian friend, don't close your mind or your heart after reading or hearing the word leadership, or leader, which discomforts many Christians. This is more common with the Hispanic or Latin American churches because many use the Reina Valera 1960 translation. Because of the fact that the Reina Valera 1960 BibleVersion does not use the word "Leader". Although I want to tell you that the Spanish Bible translation Traduccion Lengua Actual does include the word "Leader" more than one hundred times. Although some translations don't include the word "Leader", through the revelation you will be able to find the essence of the word and characteristics of a "Leader".

(Numbers 11:25):New Living Translation (NLT)

"And the Lord came down in the cloud and spoke to Moses. Then he gave the 70 elders the same spirit that was upon Moses. And when the Spirit rested upon them, the prophesied. But this never happened again."

The main point of the " I ", is the one we need to conquer, my dear reader. Since God was very clear in telling his disciples, "If any desires to come after Me, let him deny himself, and take up his cross, and follow me." (Read Matthew 16:24)(NIV)

Our leader Jesus Christ teaches us, if you want to follow my steps as a supernatural leader, and work for the company of the kingdom, you will need to, number one: neglect yourself. In other words you will need to let go of your " I ". Before conquering the world, conquer yourself. In one of the chapters I will speak about identity, and you will have the tools of the power to conquer your " I ". (Read Galatians 2:20)(NIV)

The key verse to undertake supernatural leadership is: Matthew 20:28 NKJV

"just as the Son of Man did not come to be served, but to serve, and to give His life a ransom for many." This scripture will be fundamental for a supernatural leader.

Many times we declare to God, "give me something to undertake in your kingdom", and God answers your prayer, and what he gives you is a seed. And how many times do we not understand it, because what we expected was a tree or the fruit. It seems like we don't like the process. But remember that God gives the seed to those that sow, 2Corinthians 9:10. NIV

How many times have you found yourself waiting for the final product from God, but the word of God says that faith without works is dead, (James 2:14-26) NIV. God gives you the faith, but you need to do the work and take the first step.

The growth of a leader will never be a coincidence. Let's look at the example of Joshua, God tells him, Be Brave and courages, and he orders him to stand, and to pass to the other side. You will have to do the same, In a few words God gives the promise, and you work with faith. Since faith and works always go hand in hand, (Joshua chapter 1). If we look at the case of Israel when they crossed the Jordan, this river did not open until the high priests stepped in the water and wet his feet, (Joshua chapter 3).

*2. **Traditionalism**. Do not let traditionalism, culture, dogmas and the close-minded ideas prevent the revelation of the Holy Spirit to capacitate us with the tools needed to impact, influence, and guide this generation to true success, which is for others to have a personal encounter with their creator.*

Traditionalism, in the history of philosophy, is the tendency to value tradition in conjunction with the norms and customs inherited from the past.

Tradition consists of repeating or imitating what our ancestors would have done. A principle question of tradition, as understood, is translated as building a home, when to sow and when to reap, how to dress up to go to church on Sundays, etc. Traditions are subject to change as a result of an accumulation of imperfect replicas, unless external forces impede the deviation, due to the activity in question, that variates by moments before. Let's understand that there are good traditions, but be careful with traditionalism.

Traditionalism: deliberate imitation of an original model, it is not subject to change, if traditionalism made a change while coping a model, that change would not pass the next generation that will remit to the original before the copy. Tradition as a short term memory, as opposed to traditionalism, which has a long term memory. Generally traditionalism is sustained by social norms. Tradition tends to be supported by a norm (like in the case of saying how should someone dress to attend church) but not necessarily.

A person that deviates from tradition, in technical terms for example, are you considered to be dumb or eccentric by your neighbors, but in no way a transgressor.

Traditionalism in the church has created great persecution, division, destruction, for example the time of the famous Inquisition. trying to break the innovation can also cause the revelation to be affected, wanting to maintain a custom or a dogma can stop the growth.

A dogma is a proposition that sits as firm and certain, and as an undeniable principle. Nevertheless, its most common sense is the one of a doctrine sustained by religion, or another organization of authority that does not admit replicas, it's like saying, an individual belief or collective belief not subject to test of veracity, which its contents can be religious, philosophical, social, etc., impulsed by practical utility.

I find that dogmas are more human ideologies and not so much divine revelation backed up by the gospel. Dogmatic rules are a danger in any place, let's be people that are wise and spiritual.

(Romans 12:2, 2 Corinthians 10;1-5, Philippians 3:1-14)

It was the same traditionalism that took so many people to homicide in the history of humanity.

I have experimented things in the past time, like taking a new soul to church and the Pastor of the church, himself, kicking out my guest, because he did not want to take off his hat on his first day that he had ever been to church, it was hard to speak to him again of the gospel.

I got to live through hard times and see some churches not accept the moving of the Holy Spirit, or worship with electronic instruments, or dancing, and new songs that were not accepted by traditionalists in the church, as a consequence I saw many people of my generation not want anything to do with Christ or the Church.

My dear readers, there were extreme situations, like how you couldn't be a Christian if you had a beard, had no tie, without sleeves, or couldn't wear certain types of attire, don't study or prepare yourself secularly, and I could keep giving you examples, but instead I want to speak to you about the powerful movement of the Holy Spirit, of which God prepared to be poured out on our generation. God has given me the opportunity to rejoice in the power of the Holy Spirit from my youth, and I have been able to see that the church that is growing and impacting the nations, are the ones that have the (multiform freshening wisdom of God), that only comes by the Holy Spirit. (Read all of chapter 3 of Ephesians).

Traditionalism can be a mental force in any individual and as a consequence we will have a failed person that is bonded to the past. This area is very important because many people struggle, and struggle, and never change, they pray and they pray, but there is no change. They read the bible, they prepare, they go to school, etc. but they never move forward.They can never have success when confronting their enemy. I will use the famous example of the elephant in the circus. Have you noticed that in many circuses you see the giant elephants tied with a simple rope to the dirt, and the elephant never moves from his place. The reason for this is that when the circus elephant was small, they tied him by a chain to the ground, which formed and created in his mind a custom or a permanent thought, That every time he feels something tied to his foot, he doesn't fight to get loose, or run away because years back he tried and he failed various times, but what he hasn't discerned is that he is much stronger now; and what was once a chain is now only a rope on his foot. Now, when I see in television that an elephant ran out of the circus and entered the streets of the city, I think to myself!wow!, there you have one that decided to try again, testing the innovation of a new day. God even says that his mercies are new every morning. Forgive the example or comparison, but we are not very different from the elephant. God wants you to become free of all bad habits of the past and he wants you to let go of your old self (the old man), your old ways of living, old rudiments, like Apostle Paul said. (Hebrews 6)

Lamentations 3:22-23. New King James Version "Through the Lord's mercies we are not consumed,Because His compassions fail not.They are new every morning;Great is Your faithfulness."

Ephesians 4:22-24. New King James Version "that you put off, concerning your former conduct, the old man which grows corrupt according to the deceitful lusts, and be renewed in the spirit of your mind, and that you put on the new man which was created according to God, in true righteousness and holiness."

3. **The Cains**: are an example of those who get bothered when corrected; having the opportunity to make changes, they prefer to rebel and kill the dreams of others who are approved to succeed.

Beware of this enemy because rather than a real character in the Bible it's a spirit of death, a stream of violence that goes against everything that is God's way. It is opposition to the truth and the true worship of God, and this type of people are sadly in companies, families, churches etc. They are those who share or have been part of your story, but at some point deviate from good, pure and most importantly, what is right. and for the love of another are corrected, they are exhorted to do right but their heart filled with envy, let the bad intentions of their heart become murderers of dreams, visions and goals. Instead of accepting their mistake, they prefer to rebel, trying to ruin the plan of their colleagues, followers, or brothers.

The Cains can not support to see your sacrifice and be blessed, because as Abel, says the Word, gave his first fruits and the most fattened sheep, God looked at Abel and his offering with favor, but did not look at Cains offering with favor.

A great biblical principle is this, that supernatural leaders works first on themselves before working on other people. God looks first to the heart before the offering, because if a person does the right thing or the ordinance of God, then it is sure that the offering will be the correct one, the fruit shall be correct, the result will be correct, etc.

Unfortunately, Cains are brothers that being older, should be of good example, they do not like the process nor the forms of God, they do not seek what God established, but their famous phrase is I do it my way, and I do not need anyone to teach me, I don't need anyones covering, I'd rather not give account to anyone, and I will take and give only what I see fit.

They forgot that their birth was the will of the Father, as Eve said, "I have conceived a child by the will of the the Lord", as is so, many ministries' spiritual children abandon their roots because they want to do everything their way. When in this story of the Bible we see that God himself dressed man with skins, it is He, Himself who makes the first sacrifice, and leaving a knowledge that without sacrifice there is no redemption.

With just a few words, the biggest mistake that leads the Cains to this position of failure, is that they have not understood the **priorities** in their lives, God must be first in your life looking for the Kingdom of **God** first, then the **family**, including your personal life.What does it serve a man to gain the whole world and lose his own soul. then comes the **ministry**, or vocation or work, bringing the three into one communion, without one hindering the other, only a supernatural leader can achieve this.

Cain is the first human being who commits murder, killing his brother, because of the envy he had towards him, be careful my brother do not let what happened to Cain, happen to you, that brought him the worst thing that could happen to a human, the curse of not prospering in everything that he undertook.

Abel is the kind of supernatural leader who though dead, his blood still spoke of the legacy he left here on earth, because of his sacrifice that pleased God. Abel reminds us and symbolizes Jesus Christ, leaving us his sacrifice as an example of redemption for all mankind.A Supernatural leader must be like this, his personal sacrifice will always be a blessing for many.

The most successful companies are those in which its directors always look first for benefits of the workers or employees and always think of the consumer or needy, since the supply of a good product with the right treatment will make a successful demand of progress and steady growth. (Read Acts 2: 43-47)

It is sad to see Churches with good word, but bad character. The product is good but the worker is bad, nobody wants to invest. The food is good but the waiter is bad, nobody will eat there.

I ask you,what would have happened if Cain had changed his attitude, and had done the right thing?

4. *The Judas**: are those who betray you, and the main reason is always money, they love you but they love money more, fame, recognition, comfort, and always take shortcuts in the ministry.The problem is that they blind themselves in such a way that they don't know that their decision will end with their own dreams.*

If you are a leader, there are 4 types of relations you will interact with, and one of those relationships are the:

1. **Confidants or unconditional**: these are those who love you unconditionally, and are with you in good times and bad times when you're up or you're down. They are there for you always. they are able to visit you in the hospital if you get sick, or will go see you in jail even if you were wrong. You can share with them your secrets, or whatever, because no matter your situation they are always with you and for you. They are those who will tell you the truth always, but never betray you, even though

you are wrong. They will always respect you because they love you. If you have someone like that, take care of them because there will be too few like that whom you will find in a lifetime. If you have 3 or more of them you are a blessed leader .

#2. Constituents: are those who are not with you, but are there because of what you produce; let me explain, they will work on your side while your work is important to them or has importance to them, or what they need you have, but be careful not to confuse them with the Confidential or the fact that they are there, because they are not. For when you do what no longer suits them, they will depart from you, or when you tell them your dreams and they are not in harmony with your dreams they will abandon you without any remorse in their heart. They are never with you for what you are, but for what you do. Remember that the day they find another that does what is convenient for them, they will leave you. But you know that they helped you and you were able to work with them through out the time they were with you, and thank God for them do not let your heart be sad, because they were not unconditionals.

#3.Comrades: are those who are not for you nor with you, nor for what you do, but they have the same enemy, they are against what you're against; they will engage you and form a team with you until you have helped them defeat their bigger enemy. They will be working on your side until they have seen their victory realized, then they will go, but do not be bothered or upset by the Constituents or with the Comrades, because after all if they leave, the mission will still be completed.

#4. The Judas: are those who for a long time you thought were unconditional, and maybe they were, but fell into the temptation of the material and did not know how to value your friendship and your example as a leader. The saddest thing about this is that these by their ambition end up betraying you. Giving your enemies or competitors all your information and speak what they should not of what at one day you entrusted them with, since they know your heart, and know where to attack you. As my pastor always says,"Don't worry about the Judas because they always end up hanging themselves"; ouch! How ugly, but it is the truth, as they lose their position, their friends and their reputation, conscience pursues them and eventually end their own dreams and no one else gives them the trust again. The problem of the Judas is that they don't seek the necessary help to be able to stand up again, but fall on their own personal self-destruction plans, until they reach failure. The only thing is that the relationships with a Judas impel you to accelerate your calling or mission to another level after they have attacked you, you will always come out triumphant, if you keep your posture as a great leader of example.A leader that would never do what he doesn't want done to him. Treat others how you want to be treated, this is the motto of one who does not walk by sight but by their faith, because the more damage they have done to you, you will never sow what do not want to reap.

#5. Dictators or Sauls: *are bad leaders who can not stand to see one of their constituents progress or improve their status of a ministry, or a company, or a corporation; and instead of turning that person into an ally, and teach them the fundamentals of the kingdom or the company, they tend to try to get them out of business or ministerial box. Chasing them until they see them flee. In this point we need to, as good leaders, always take inventory of our own lives or ministry and examine ourselves, asking these questions: how are we directing?, How much have we grown?, What has been the result of the system I'm using?, and what influence do I have on those that follow me?, because the good leader, will always be a good example for others and a man of influence. This is where leaders differentiate from each other. There are those who are dictators; they have a mentality of position, because someone put them as the boss they believe that everyone must blindly obey their orders, and to a certain extent they have some reason to believe that all those who are under their power must obey. This is what we call a dictatorship and not a leadership, because it is very possible that this dictator or "Boss" will soon reach the point where he will only have employees and not followers or people wanting to reproduce what their leader has inspired in them.*

Usually the dictator is afraid that someone will take their place and therefore never reproduces in his followers, and much less recognize the virtues of his followers or employees, that is why the Sauls or dictators do not have a legacy, their reign ends when they die, or leave, and it is sad to see churches, ministries, companies, sports teams, marching bands, that always end because the leader never left a legacy to those who came after them whether it be their children or the closest ones to them.

Saul being king persecuted David a young man conformed to the heart of God, instead of recognizing his virtues, he ended up feeling envious, to the point of kicking him out of the kingdom, not knowing that David would soon be the new King of Israel. It would have been better for Saul to recognize his weakness and make an alliance with David, since they were both from the same Kingdom, together they could have done more than divided. Jesus said, a kingdom divided against itself can not stand (Matthew 12:25).

A Supernatural leader, always works with a team, and recognizes the virtues of his followers.

Practice the following points and you'll be a successful leader:

1. NEVER STOP CAPACITATING YOURSELF
2. PLAN THE VISION AND UNDERTAKE YOUR CALLING.
3. FORM A TEAM.
4. NEVER WORK ALONE, ALWAYS HAVE A MENTOR.
5. RECOGNIZE THE VIRTUES OF YOUR FOLLOWERS.
6. DELEGATE YOUR LEADERSHIP AND SHARE THE WORK.
7. NEVER DO ALL THE WORK, HAVE ASSOCIATES.
8. PROMOTE THOSE THAT DO IT WELL.
9. ALWAYS TEACH AND REPRODUCE IN OTHERS.
10. ALWAYS LEAVE A LEGACY OR SUCCESSOR.

The biggest example is found in the Bible, all the men who triumphed in their calling had successors, like Abraham, Isaac and Jacob, or like Elijah and Elisha, or like David and Solomon, and Jesus Christ who left the Church the biggest legacy of salvation, and thus the Church must give by grace what by grace has received.

CHAPTER 3

TRAINED AND CALLED FOR LEADERSHIP

Romans 12: 6-8

King James Version (NKJV)

"**6** Having then gifts differing **according to the grace** that is given to us, *let us use them:* if prophecy, *let us prophesy* in proportion to our faith; **7** or ministry, *let us use it* in *our* ministering; he who teaches, in teaching; **8** he who exhorts, in exhortation; he who gives, with liberality; **he who leads**, with diligence; he who shows mercy, with cheerfulness."

New Living Translation (NLT)

"**6** In his grace, God has given us different gifts for doing certain things well. So if God has given you the ability to prophesy, speak out with as much faith as God has given you. **7** If your gift is serving others, serve them well. If you are a teacher, teach well. **8** If your gift is to encourage others, be encouraging. If it is giving, give generously. If God has given you **leadership ability**, take the responsibility seriously. And if you have a gift for showing kindness to others, do it gladly."

King James Version (KJV)

"**6** Having then gifts differing **according to the grace** that is given to us, whether prophecy, let us prophesy according to the proportion of faith; **7** Or ministry, let us wait on our ministering: or he that teacheth, on teaching;

8 Or he that exhorteth, on exhortation: he that giveth, let him do it with simplicity; he that ruleth, with diligence; he that sheweth mercy, with cheerfulness."

When we talk about gifts, talents and abilities, we talk about all the skills a child of God has to take on leadership. These skills are like tools for someone who edifies, for someone who builds, for someone who works in ministry, in other words, everybody needs tools. The mechanic needs tools to fix a car, the gardener needs tools for pruning and gardening. The doctor needs tools to operate and save a life from death. The Christian leader is one who uses all the possible tools at his reach to compose and fix, operate and save a life from spiritual death and even sometimes from physical death. This means that while many work only with the earthly, God has allowed us to work with the eternal, therefore our responsibility is much greater than that of a doctor when it comes to a life; a life is a soul, and Jesus said, "For what profit is it to a man if he gains the whole world, and loses his own soul? Or what will a man give in exchange for his soul" (Matthew 16:26)NIV. This lets us know the value of the soul for Jesus.

This is where supernatural leadership is born, because a Christian that values and understands this, will ask the Holy Spirit to open their mind and their heart to know what is his perfect and pleasing will to reach lost souls of this generation, then we will be able to hear the calling to enable us to learn and always be on the level that supernatural leadership demands. (See Romans 12: 2)

Every Supernatural leader needs to be free to enter the dimension of the Spirit where everything is possible.

There are tools that are obtained at birth, but there are others that are acquired during our growth.

To acquire one of these tools you have to know how to invest. It is probable that you were not born a prophet, but if you invest in prayer God will reveal what your eyes have not yet seen, and he will give you the plan, the design and the vision for what you are undertaking.

(Luke 14: 28) King James Version (KJV)
"For which of you, intending to build a tower, sitteth not down first, and counteth the cost, whether he have sufficient to finish it?"

(Jeremiah 33: 3) King James Version (KJV)
"Call unto me, and I will answer thee, and show thee great and mighty things, which thou knowest not."

Probably you were not born with the gift of faith, but if you invest your time in reading and hearing the word of God, faith will come and be activated in your life to receive more faith.

(Romans 10:17) King James Version (KJV)
"So then faith cometh by hearing, and hearing by the word of God."

If someone lacks something ask for it, long for it, desire it, search for it, and snatch it because the work of the God's kingdom will be established and unleashed on earth by those who have decided to constantly capacitate and prepare themselves to be ready for the calling to go and make disciples of all the nations. For this reason, the Apostle Paul, a man who was very used by God, author of the majority of books of the New Testament, teacher of nations, evangelist of the gentiles, and a man used in the gifts of the Holy Spirit and the power of the Word. The reason is because God used all of his capacity taking his ministry to an exemplary leadership capacity.

(James 1: 5 KJV) "If any of you lack wisdom, let him ask of God, that giveth to all men liberally, and up braideth not; and it shall be given him."

(Matthew 11:12 NLT) "And from the time John the Baptist began preaching until now, the Kingdom of Heaven has been forcefully advancing,[a] and violent people are attacking it."

(1 Corinthians 12:31KJV) "But covet earnestly the best gifts: and yet show I unto you a more excellent way."

There are no valid excuses we can all undertake leadership,if you have life, you can do it. The question that many people ask themselves is: Are leaders born or made?

Truth is that we make this question many times, because we are afraid to make mistakes, undertaking a leadership that can fail. But know something, I'd prefer to try it than to never undertake it because of fear of failure. John C. Maxwell would say we were all born and until this day there isn't a leader that was not born, but we know that a leader can learn to be, if he proposes it and capacitates himself. I ask you a question: Are leaders built up for the role or play the role?As we would say in Mexico, there are those that are made leaders, and those that play the role, but do nothing.

In other words start today, capacitate yourself today, train today, practice today, embark today, tomorrow may be too late.

One of the biggest excuses among the "spiritual people" is that "I do not need anyone to show me because Jesus said the Holy Spirit will show me all things; but this truth can be misinterpreted if hermeneutics is not used.If we go to the context, the Bible also teaches that the same Holy Spirit established, 5 ministries, among which is the Masters Jesus. Therefore dear readers, we all need to be taught and we need to find someone who can teach us and prepare us, wether it be in Sunday school, Bible colleges, universities, etc. (Ephesians 4:11)

WE UNDERSTAND THAT THE LARGEST TRAINING KNOWLEDGE AND WISDOM, COME FROM GOD.

Hosea 4:6King James Version (KJV)
6 My people are destroyed for lack of knowledge: because thou hast rejected knowledge, I will also reject thee, that thou shalt be no priest to me: seeing thou hast forgotten the law of thy God, I will also forget thy children.

WISDOM

Proverbs 18:15New King James Version (NKJV
The heart of the prudent acquires knowledge, And the ear of the wise seeks knowledge.

"Learning is remembering what you know, acting is to demonstrate what you know,, Richard Bach

"I would give all I know for half of what I ignore" René Descartes

The wise lacks nothing, however needs many things,on the contrary, the fool does not need anything, because he doesn't know how to use anything, but lacks everything."Crispo"

The wise never say everything he thinks, but always thinks everything he says "Aristoteles"

Let the wise not feel to mourn, but gets merrily to his task of repairing the damage done "William Shakespeare"

It's better to be corrected by a wise man, than It is to be admired by a fool. Platon

"The doors of wisdom are never closed" Benjamin Franklin

"Its not enough to know, you also have to apply. It is not enough to want, we must also act" Johann Wolfgang von Goethe

CHAPTER 4

WITHOUT IDENTITY THERE IS NO AUTHORITY

A biblical principle that we can not ignore is that of the authority,we can never accept or understand these biblical principles if we have no identity, of which the order is, if I have identity, i have honor, and if I have honor, i have authority. (Matthew 7: 28-29) Mark 6:2) (Matthew 28:18) Jesus knew and understood his identity as Son and so he fought for his purpose up until the cross, and the Father seeing his honor in such a way that the Son always recognized he who had sent him, the Father himself gave him his glory and knowing that he was given a Name above all names. That is why he had authority, and that Authority and Glory he shared to his disciples. If we can have a summary of what is Identity to have Authority read (John chapter 17)

What is my identity? an identification card serves us to acquire all kinds of benefits, whenever you go to the bank you will need identification, or if you go to a government office you need an ID, if you want to enter another country or territory you will need an ID, also in the same manner in leadership if you want to obtain honor and authority you will have to know and be sure what your identity is . The only way to know what your identity is and were it stands is when you are in a transaction or a process, that is where you are required to reveal your true identity; only in the middle of a Test, we know who we really are. Now ask yourself(**Who am i in Christ?**)

1). I am Made in the image and likeness of God. I have the image of the almighty God, knowing that all human beings were made in the likeness of God. Giving value to others will bring value to myself, but if i never value myself, i will never be able to value others. (Genesis 1:27)

There is great power in this principle of identity, seeing the virtues of others and recognizing that they are creation of God, if you can see the creation of God in others you will be able to achieve the Commandments of God in your life.(Exodus 20)

Its curious to see that God gives Moses 10 written commandments,as a summary of the law, and if you can see the first 4 are to honor God and the other 6 are for Honoring your neighbor and yourself .It is easy to love and value God, but it is more difficult to value Gods creation and respect it because we are forgetful beings, but as of today you can start honoring your parents, not steal from your neighbor, nor covet what belongs to others, etc. Really recognize that you and I carry the image of God All Mighty and that way we will live in peace.

2). I am the son of God. Only those who have accepted Jesus and believe in Him have been given a power, authority and a legacy, to be called sons of God. I am a son and not a slave, I ask as a son and not as a beggar, I pray as a son and not as a stranger, I speak as a son and not like a bastard. (John 1: 11-12)

It is important to know that we are children of the King and not slaves, according to (Galatians 4: 1) Now I say that the heir, as long as he is a child, does not differ at all from a slave, though he is master of all, while he ignores who he is, or understands who he is, until he matures, only then could he enjoy his inheritance.

3). I am a new creature, born again. Nicodemus, a teacher of the law could not understand this, because only the one who has been born again from the waters and the spirit will be able to understand the supernatural things.You can undertake a business leadership without the spirit of God but you will never undertake a supernatural leadership if you are not born again. The supernatural of God not only conquers the earthly, but it also takes you to conquer the eternal.

Matthew 6:33New King James Version (NKJV)
33 But seek first the kingdom of God and His righteousness, and all these things shall be added to you.

2 Corinthians 5:17New King James Version (NKJV)
17 Therefore, if anyone is in Christ, he is a new creation; old things have passed away; behold, all things have become new.

All leaders need to understand that everything we are inside is reflected on the outside, you can learn to be a leader and the technics of a leadership but you will never become a supernatural leader, if you cannot conquer yourself because sooner or later you will need the most important part of a leader, which is his character.

4).I am more than conquerer. There is no weapon created or raised obstacle powerful enough to separate me from my purpose. God taught me that weapons will be forged against me, but shall not prosper. though obstacles will rise, they will not be able to separate me from his love, and there will be afflictions in this world but I must trust in him because he has overcame the world. (Romanos 8:28-39)

5). I am someone that can do everything in Christ. The culture of fear is constantly dragging our generation, through advertising that occurs in media such as television, the radio, the Internet, science, politics, etc. It is sad to see that products are sold through the culture of fear, fear of getting sick, afraid to not grow, fear to not prosper, fear of failure, fear of losing, many want to sell or get something through fear. Cults want to win members instilling fear to their followers, why go so far! There are parents that only know how to earn the respect of their own instilling fear with clamor, threats and even blows. Our enemy has raised a spirit of fear, so the supernatural leaders hide their talents and abilities, here are two promises on behalf of God, which if you apply them,you will have success.

Philippians 4:11-13New King James Version (NKJV)
11 Not that I speak in regard to need, for I have learned in whatever state I am, to be content: 12 I know how to be abased, and I know how to abound. Everywhere and in all things I have learned both to be full and to be hungry, both to abound and to suffer need. 13 I can do all things through Christ[a] who strengthens me.

2 Timothy 1:7New King James Version (NKJV)
7 For God has not given us a spirit of fear, but of power and of love and of a sound mind.

CHAPTER 5

17 CHARACTERISTICS OF A SUPERNATURAL LEADER

The Bible gives us a powerful reference on characters of a leader, and he is one of the most influential apostles in history, of who being the spiritual father and mentor of the young pastorTimothy, through this letter he reveals the importance of the character of a Leader, teaching us in (1 Timothy 3) the following:

faithful saying: If a man desires the episcopate, good work he desires

1. *faithful word, means that this word never fails.*
2. *If a man desire episcopate, means that we can all reach a level of leadership, and the key is to yearn.*
3. *You desire a good work, means that the decision taken will be productive but it takes work, action, effort and service.*

Bishop *comes from Greek (episkopos, (from Latin episcopus, in Greek émiokomoc, watcher, inspector, oversee, overseer, a leader, or someone exercising leadership.*

This term reveals the character of the leaders of the church, whose mission is to help the faithful of the congregation to get 3 principles

1. *that they might know the gifts the Lord gives (Eph. 4: 7-8)*
2. *implement them. (James 1: 21-25)*
3. *comply each day with their homework better. (Matthew 28: 19-20)*

1).To be blameless, *that their behavior does not lead to human repression or reproach of any sort. This word leads us to the three parts of the a human being, spirit,soul,and body; in this case it requires that the leader is man or woman with the right attitudes, good fruit, healthy thoughts and mentalities; in short, the leader should be a good example. Being blameless from Greek (ANEPILEMPTOS)speaks of someone who has nothing that an opponent can take away; of which can base an accusation. This word here seems to be a general description of characteristics of a bishop. Proverbs*

4:18New King James Version (NKJV)18 But the path of the just is like the shining sun,[a]That shines ever brighter unto the perfect day.

2).husband to one women. *The text appears to indicate not to be polygamous, but the full meaning is much wider and can not be limited to polygamy.*

Not only do you marry physically but also mentally, and fantasizing about other women or flirting with them, can not be considered as being a husband of one wife.

It can also refer to those that are divorced and remarried. which In my personal opinion, it is very difficult for a leader like that to be teaching about marriage, if you have already had several failures, their example to our generation will not be adequate. In these days people take marriage as something that gets old and out of style and that is a serious mistake, because marriage is a foundation for society and a very important biblical principle.

Praise God for those leaders who can maintain and reach success in their first marriage and remain to inspire others while with teaching them with example.Since there are many who have wanted to dilute this requisite and quality that every leader should have, only one wife in this life and not one wife at a time.

Dear Reader I want to take this time to tell you that you can live and enjoy a happy marriage your whole life. despite the difficulties that come it is worthwhile to go through them and maintain the love that joined you as a couple, forever until death do us part.

Our Generation urgently needs Marriage models. Mainly in the Church because this is no longer outside the church but within the church, we cannot stand by and loose our fundamentals, because the building can weaken and fall.

Those that tend to a church, must take care of their Family equally. not one before the other, but both together.Perhaps we could say that the church is first, but considering that the family is also part of that church, this is for parents who are supernatural leaders.

advice read: Matthew 19: 1-12.Jesus taught about divorce.

*3). **Sober.** We could understand as moderation the eating and drinking, but Paul goes further. Sobriety is the state of mind that one is free from the excessive influence of passion greed or emotions. Paul uses the greek term**(NEFALIOS)**, which gives the idea of self-control, someone careful, as in the case of Daniel. Sobriety should be in all aspects of life .How many of us that are involved in the ministry find so many different types of imprudent people who believe they are leaders.But when you get to talk to them, of the abundance of the heart the mouth speaks, you will know their interest, their weaknesses, their priorities, but it is sad to find people with such a lack of sobriety in speech, an incredible lack of ministerial ethics, such as the vulgarities, red jokes, gossip, even of their mentors or colleagues, etc., lack of sobriety even in their eyes. It is important that every leader is sober, to do things with freedom and never with debauchery.*

*4). **Prudent,** sensible, discreet, wise to avoid faults and dangers*

Matthew 10:16New King James Version (NKJV)
16 "Behold, I send you out as sheep in the midst of wolves. Therefore be wise as serpents and harmless as doves.

*Prudence (Greek **frenesis** of fronéo. "I have trial, I think rightly, i advise, in Latin prudentia, of providens) it is from the old, a skill linked to the praxis (practice), the virtuous ability to regulate so conveniently and orderly the actions to achieve a stated purpose.*

Prudence is another virtue much needed in Leadership, as the Bible says reckless woman with her own hands destroys her house.The imprudent virgins did not have enough oil for their lamps to wait for the husband. We can commit so much destruction and offenses all due to lacking prudence .For example, some leaders are not discreet or prudent while they cant keep information or secrets of things that have happened and they share it openly in their public meetings, giving names and details, which will be a disappointment for his followers.

The leader knows his audience before speaking, knows how to dress for different occasions, and strives to have a plan before embarking on his/her objective, in other words he knows both ends and knows just how stay in boundary without affecting others to achieve a purpose.

5). Decent. Decent is synonymous with modesty, purity and honesty. Platon would say that the decorous person (Greek **kosmios**) is one that without flaunting fulfill his duties as a citizen and does it tidily.

Kosmios is who puts limitations on their own freedom.

Being Decorous speaks of a habit, something you can put on, knowing that habits can become virtues. This Greek word speaks of practicing honesty, seeking the good for those who are watching us.

1 Corinthians 10:23-24New King James Version (NKJV)
23 All things are lawful for me,[a] but not all things are helpful; all things are lawful for me,[b] but not all things edify. 24 Let no one seek his own, but each one the other's well-being.

6). Host. The Greek term **Filoxenos** originally meant love strangers, and then I include the sense of those who are pleased to give hospitality. In the first century often Christians were homeless on account of the persecution, the bishop was to show compassion in those cases. Moreover, the bishops were to receive in their home the brothers when they were traveling and they needed a place to spend the night. looking back to Acts 13: 2 Paul was declaring that the bishops should rejoice opening their homes to others.

7).*worthy to teach.**Maybe Paul did not think that all were capable of speaking in the congregations. but did believe everyone was capable to teach in a simple way the will of God for daily living. Suitable for teaching, involves both the capacity to teach the truth but also to refute the error.Every leaders needs to be prepared,equipped, and trained to teach others, because the desire of every good leader is to impart on others their knowledge and shape a vision in his followers.This is achieved through teaching. Jesus said in Matthew 28:19 and 20 go and make disciples to all the nations, and then he tells them how* *to do it, he tells them teaching them, this means that a good teacher will never stop teaching and never stop learning and stays innovative.*

8). Not given to wine. *Here it refers to not get drunk, which would always be improper for a worker of the Lord. The sin of drunkenness carries many others, such as immorality, profanity, shamelessness, litigation, pride, etc. (Habakkuk 2: 5) (Ephesians 5:18)*

Not given to much wine. *In this epistle 1 Timothy 3, three kinds of people are mentioned and their relationship with wine: The bishop, who is ordered not to be given to wine (3: 3); The deacon, to which Paul asks to not be given to much wine (3: 8); the young shepherd, whom the apostle recommends takes a little wine because of his continuous stomach diseases (5:23). The question of wine, we must understand establishing some general principles in this regard:*

1. *God condemns drunkenness (1 Corinthians 6: 9-10)*
2. *God speaks of drinking wine and does not mention other alcoholic beverages There are many who, taking into account these passages, the same as John 2 where Christ turns the water into wine, indulge in all sorts of binge drinking, drinking concoctions, beer, mezcal, and other intoxicating teas.*
3. *Who is recommended to drink wine, it is done because of the incapacity to drink water. Not everywhere in the word he water is suitable for some peoples sensitive stomachs.*
4. *When the Bible says drink wine, it then says "use a little"*
5. *God commands Christians that if they eat or drink or do anything else, do it all for the glory of God (1 Cor 10:31). Before drinking, be sure that with it we can glorify the Lord.*
6. *Although the Bible allows me to take some wine (if so we interpret it that way), before doing so I consider that if the food to my brother is a stumble, I will never eat meat, so as not to offend my brother (1 C.8: 13)*
7. *There are so many alcoholics in our world, and many children who can be influenced by bad example, it would be best to abstain from all alcoholic drinks whether it is much or a little.*

I will always remember some of my relatives may they rest in peace, as child, i remember the family saying to them, don't drink anymore, unfortunately they died, from torn livers, but the same ones saying don't drink anymore were the ones making them stumble in this addiction. Those who drank "socially" as they used to say fancied those that were weak and caused them to fall into the addiction once again drinking for days even months without stopping, until they were killed by their addiction .

9).not quarrelsome. *Although excess wine often produces a quarrelsome spirit, it is also possible to be a fighter without being dedicated to drinking. being quarrelsome not only refers to violence that reaches punches, but to those of words. Paul declares himself against fables and genealogies [that] carry Disputes (1 Timothy 1: 3-4), questions and strifes of words (1 Timothy 6:4), that are vain and without point.there are people who love to quarrel in front of others to show people what they know. Nobody wants to know, or listen to what you know, until they look at your works, and if you are one of those who believe that you know everything or that your always correct and thinks everyone else is wrong, except you. Those who think like that will be bad leaders that are evaded, and no one will want to share their views or opinions with you.of which will weaken your leadership and you will never get the confidence of those who follow you or those who work for your vision.*

10). not a filthy lucre. The apostle is not against profits, which are God prized to those that sows and works. The exhortation here is to those who seek it dishonesty and often with injustice and lies.unfortunately there will always be Judas in our midst. The youth poet, stated: "He who wishes to get rich, wishes to get rich quickly." And the warning about the dangers of those that want to get rich, the letter speaks brilliantly in l Timothy 6: 9-10. of those who obtains dishonest earnings?

(A) Any person who lends money with usury (Exodus 22:25)
(B)those that obtained profits with church money (Acts 5: 3);
(C) those that don't render clear accounts (2 Chronicles 24:11);
(D) those that keep the churches money (2 Kings 12:15)

Greed is the excessive desire for wealth, without wanting to treasure them. If you are a person who constantly wants things others have and they are not necessities, it is likely that you can fall into greed of dishonest earnings, using tactics, cunning habits, bad habits to be implying to others to give to you, that they may let you borrow, that they may invite you, that they may take you, inventing false needs so they may supply for you. Let it be God Himself, who supplies all your needs according to his riches in glory, leaving the manipulation aside and letting the Holy Spirit be the one who guides people to bless, believe there will be no limits. (Philippians 4:19)

11). But kind: affectionate, gentle, pleasant and helpful. n Greek it is **EPIEIKES**

EPI meaning into and **EIKOS** means gladly. The word suggests a fair, reasonable, patient, moderate, fair and considered character. It is the opposite of rough, hurtful, sarcastic, cruel and contentious. The person with a **EPIEIKES** character does not insist on the letter of the law

12). Peaceful, calm and quiet, opposite quarrelsome. The definition of the Greek word **Esuquios** (peaceful)

13). Not a penny pincher.penny pinchers are those who want more than they need, love money and want to get rich. They are ambitious and greedy, they are always dissatisfied and are unhappy. They are often precisely those who seek filthy lucre.

14). must manage his home well. Although the Deacons are also asked to manage well his household, the comment is not added to the bishop (If anyone does not know how to rule his own house, then how can he take care of God's church?). And with this timely clarification it defines the principal responsibility of a bishop or leader of a congregation: to govern and take care of Gods church.The word "Elder" is found 30 times in the book of Acts and the Epistles, material that narrates the beginning, organization and recommendations to the church of Christ. Your home is your family and all things that are under your care something that every good leader must have is a good judgment of his government. And the best fruit of good leadership is to see his home serving, in this case in the Church, ministering and subject to the same Pastor. It is sad to hear when someone complains, because the family of the Pastor has many places of service in the church, I truly believe that this is something that is good and not bad, because what would be better, would it be better for people to say that the Pastor's family is lost,and that none come to church, or to see them involved in the same vision, personally when someone tells me, pastor well done, i receive it like a normal compliment, because they do not completely know me in the intimate, but when someone in my family honors me with those words, glory to God because they really know me outside the church and in the intimate, or for your wife to tell you, well done or you're a good leader and I'm happy for your example, that is really where the testimony of your government takes more value.

15). Have your children obey. The subjection that the children show should reflect the character of the Fathers leadership. Furthermore, Paul probably had in mind a look at the parent-child and child-parent relationship, from both sides. There would be submission from the children, and a serious and careful leadership of the father. I think the success of a leader begins at home, and we will always have this saying, healthy families will be the result of a healthy church and a healthy church will have growth. The Example of a leader to others, will be successful when others can see that your children enjoy having a parent like you. You can succeed in finances, or have success in the spiritual, or even have success in entrepreneurship, but if you can not enjoy that success with your children, it is not true success. True leaders do not make their followers submit, but they act in a way that makes the Followers want to submit to them.

16).Not A neophyte. This word refers to a new convert, a novice. In a religion or someone newly admitted to a Party is considered neophyte. In Greek **Neofytos,** means recently planted.Leadership should not be left in the hands of amateurs who just initiated. One of the keys is that Jesus himself says in the parable of the talents that he gave to each of his servants according to his capacity, not only means that God demands according to what is given to us, but also we need to understand that God will not entrust something to someone who is not capable, and one of the worst mistakes in the Church, Companies, Organizations, is that people are put in places that people still are not trained to perform the job right. It is awful to have someone who does not know anything about music conducting the music worship or singing in a church, or a preacher who does not show up prepared for his message the day of service, or an usher that can't give a greeting at the door of the church. Someone who was not instructed will be easily destroyed. This biblical passage says in"

1 Timothy 3:6 (NKJV)
6 not a novice, lest being puffed up with pride he fall into the *same* condemnation as the devil.

The great danger for the neophyte is to fall into vanity. Usually, a novice who suddenly receives an important position thinks more in the honor he will receive than the service to be rendered, and is easy to become conceited, filled with the smoke of pride, and exposed to the fall in the same condemnation that the devil fell.he will be a hindrance rather than a help, instead will bring disorders rather than edification to the church, and could witness shame. It is good to remember

Proverbs 16:18 (NKJV)
18 Pride *goes* before destruction, And a haughty spirit before a fall.

17).good testimony from those outside. When a Christian has a bad testimony outside the church and still receives an important position in the church, it is like saying we don't care of your misconduct; You can take charge and "We do not mind you behaving in the same way." A person like that will have no interest in changing their behavior.

Plus, tolerance in this sense comes into contradiction with the first of the bishops requirements, to be above reproach.

without duplicity. They should not be skittish or speak with double meanings but be people of one word, firm in what they say and do. An example of a faithful man was the deacon Stephen, that even when he was stoned he stood firm in his Christian convictions, and he prayed to God for his executors.(Acts 7:60)

There is nothing worse than a double-minded leader (James 1: 8 says in the Bible that *he is* unstable in all his ways.

Somedays Joyful, other day Embittered, these are men who live by circumstances and not by faith, in other words the circumstances empower them and not them over their circumstances.The righteous walks by faith and not by sight, and the righteous shall live by faith. (Habakkuk 2: 4) (2 Corinthians 5: 7).

CHAPTER 6

THE PRAYER OF A LEADER

Everything starts with a prayer, before undergoing any project, implanting any vision, starting a plan, or making any decision,every leader must pray.

Nehemiah 1:3-4New King James Version (NKJV)
3 And they said to me, "The survivors who are left from the captivity in the province *are* there in great distress and reproach. The wall of Jerusalem *is* also broken down, and its gates are burned with fire."**4** So it was, when I heard these words, that I sat down and wept, and mourned *for many* days; I was fasting and praying before the God of heaven.

Nehemiah is an example of a super natural leader. Nehemiah heard the need of a leader to go and rebuild the walls and its gates of Jerusalem, this moved his heart with a great passion, he prayed before the God of the heavens.

The success in a supernatural leader lies is his trust of God, he does not rely only on his own understanding but he knows that wisdom comes from the God of hosts.

In the example of Nehemiah we can see that it was God himself that put the grace and favor in Nehemiah after he had prayed to God,It was God that opened doors and provided everything that was needed to complete the works for restoring Jerusalem.

Ezekiel 22:30-31New King James Version (NKJV)
30 So I sought for a man among them who would make a wall, and stand in the gap before Me on behalf of the land, that I should not destroy it; but I found no one. 31 Therefore I have poured out My indignation on them; I have consumed them with the fire of My wrath; and I have recompensed their deeds on their own heads," says the Lord God.

What is Prayer?

Praying is communicating with God, it is the means God left so that we can have a personal relationship with our creator.

Matthew 6:7New King James Version (NKJV)
7 And when you pray, do not use vain repetitions as the heathen *do*. For they think that they will be heard for their many words

Someone said that prayer is to speak with God, but we need to understand an important part, not only do we have to know how to speak to God, but we also need to know how to hear God.

Jeremiah 33:3New King James Version (NKJV)
3 'Call to Me, and I will answer you, and show you great and mighty things, which you do not know.'

The word of God says call unto me, calling out to him denotes that we must do it with fervor and passion, not like something monotoned but with cheer and enthusiastic to have been heard.With an expectation that he will answer and he will give us a revelation of what we need to acquire to complete our goal.he will show us what we did not know, strategies, solutions, innovations, forms and methods to achieve what others have not been able to achieve.You and i will accomplish it if we learn to listen to what God is teaching us.

Revelation comes through prayer.if a leader does not pray, he will never be able to obtain a higher spiritual level and he will never be able to have revelation from God.We need revelation, it is the means for us to get out of the test, or to find the solution to the problem, or to get to know and understand what no human being can see with natural eyes.

If you don't pray you might get to be a leader, but never a supernatural leader. The supernatural leader can see what others cant see.

Definition of the word Revelation: from the Hebrew word Gala which means to reveal with the intent to uncover or rip something out.(Isaiah 47:3)

-Apocalypse from the greek word Apokalipsis which means revealed truth or to run the vail.

lastly from the greek word Faneron which means to manifest or present.

the goal of the revelation is that we may all get to know God in a real and personal way.(get to know the secrets of God)

Luke 11:1New King James Version (NKJV)
11 Now it came to pass, as He was praying in a certain place, when He ceased, *that* one of His disciples said to Him, "Lord, teach us to pray, as John also taught his disciples."

we could scrutinize everything about prayer, but in this occasion we will only touch some important points

A disciple asked his mentor to teach them to pray.

1. The example of a leader in prayer

How many times do we go to a prayer service and unfortunately the ones that aren't there are the leaders.

personally i nick named them, "those that are always getting rides or asking for a push like they say in Mexico", these are the ones that always say "pray for me!" but they don't even pray for themselves.

The reason why the disciples asked Jesus to teach them to pray was because they observed his example.Jesus was a leader that always prayed, and every time he prayed supernatural works happened.

2. The leader should show his followers to pray

How many times have we asked someone to pray and the respond is "I don't know how to pray". It surprises us because they have been disciples in the faith for years.

This verse in Luke 11:1 shows us the need that our disciples have to learn from us the leaders, to know how to pray.It doesn't matter what ministry you serve God in, don't forget, show your followers to pray.

3. Model prayer

The lords prayer is the model prayer that Jesus christ left his disciples and it will be the model prayer for a super natural leader.

Do you believe that Jesus wanted his disciples to repeat the same thing to God when they prayed?More than a model prayer it is a divine revelation from the father to his children, and a blessing to all citizens of the kingdom of God.

The purpose of this model prayer wasn't so that it would be done repeatedly or a simple saying, but the teacher was teaching his disciples with the best method, the example.

Our father

If we say father it is because we truly are children of God, since there are many that believe that we are all children of God, unfortunately that is not true, only those that are washed by the blood of the lamb, have that dominion.I'll explain it.In reality we are all creation of God, but children are only those that have truly excepted God in their hearts and live a life according to his word.

the bible tells us:

John 1:12New King James Version (NKJV)
12 But as many as received Him, to them He gave the right to become children of God, to those who believe in His name:

These are the true children of God.those that have been begotten by him of his own will.Not by human will.The apostle paul says to the Romans that only those that are lead by the Holy spirit are children of God.

Romans 8:1New King James Version (NKJV)
8 *There is* therefore now no condemnation to those who are in Christ Jesus,[a] who do not walk according to the flesh, but according to the Spirit.

If we say we are his children, then we will do all that the father asks, and we will represent his law, his commandments, acting like children and not like beggars.The almoner only asks and asks but doesn't represent anyone, nor does he try to get out of his situation, but the children should always be obedient to their parents, like the commandment asks and they will be represented by a legacy.

In heaven

God is omnipresent, but his holy spirit lives in us, letting us know that our kingdom is not of this world, but it is from heaven, reminding us to not put our sight on the earthly things or the perishable, but unto heaven.

John 14:23New King James Version (NKJV)
23 Jesus answered and said to him, "If anyone loves Me, he will keep My word; and My Father will love him, and We will come to him and make Our home with him.

He lives in our hearts but he reminds us that there is a difference, from our earthly parents, and our heavenly father which is spirit and he will never fail us.He is in a high and sublime place and he is not like us, but he is spirit.

Although he allows us to call him father, demonstrating that he is near us, He is above everyone, and above all,THE ALL MIGHTY.

Hallowed be thy name

This is the most appropriate way to come close to God, grateful and with praise before asking for something, give thanks to him that you are before his holiness, he deserves all reverence, admiration and praise, it is sad how so many think that praying is just asking.we can seem like sheep saying give meeeeeee, supply for meeeeee, fill meeeeee, forgive meeeeeee, nourish meeeeee etc.but we should know that when we praise God we will gain more and advance more. When we praise God we give thanks before hand for what he will give us.

There are 3 types of worshipers, those that worship God for what has been given to them, those that worship him although they haven't received what they want, and lastly those that worship God always.We need to worship him for what he is.

Psalm 100New King James Version (NKJV)
1 Make a joyful shout to the Lord, all you lands!
2 Serve the Lord with gladness; Come before His presence with singing.
3 Know that the Lord, He *is* God; *It is* He *who* has made us, and not we ourselves;[a] *We are* His people and the sheep of His pasture.
4 Enter into His gates with thanksgiving, *And* into His courts with praise. Be thankful to Him, *and* bless His name.
Our teacher reminds us that our God is holy and perfect.
he says to us, be holy as i am holy.

Matthew 5:48New King James Version (NKJV)
48 Therefore you shall be perfect, just as your Father in heaven is perfect.

Never forget his commandment, his name is holy and sacred, never swear, nor curse in the name of God.Our teacher Jesus gives us an example to always pray, sanctifying the name of God.

exodus 20:7New King James Version (NKJV)
7.You shall not take the name of the Lord your God in vain, for the Lord will not hold him guiltless who takes His name in vain.

your kingdom come

here is the priority of asking for his kingdom to be established.

Matthew 6:33New King James Version (NKJV)
33 But seek first the kingdom of God and His righteousness, and all these things shall be added to you.

The teacher leaves it very clear that in our petitions we establish his kingdom, because when the lords kingdom comes the supernatural is let loose.God gives us the key to loosen the supernatural, and see the miracles happen, the impossible will be possible.This happens when we say your kingdom come and with faith we believe not doubting, it will happen.

Matthew 21:22New King James Version (NKJV)
22 And whatever things you ask in prayer, believing, you will receive."

Matthew 28:18New King James Version (NKJV)
18 And Jesus came and spoke to them, saying, "All authority has been given to Me in heaven and on earth.

when we say your kingdom come, we are inviting Jesus with all his glory to come and show us his power, since this is a battle of kingdom vs.kingdom,when we call on the kingdom of God, the kingdom of darkness will be defeated.

Acts 2:34New King James Version (NKJV)
34 "For David did not ascend into the heavens, but he says himself:

'The Lord said to my Lord, "Sit at My right hand,

Jesus has all authority in heaven as in earth and underneath the earth, but it is our turn to declare it as citizens of his kingdom, if God says it, i believe it, if i believe it God will do it, When you declare something its because you believe it.

Ephesians 1:20-22New King James Version (NKJV)
20 which He worked in Christ when He raised Him from the dead and seated *Him* at His right hand in the heavenly *places,***21** far above all principality and power and might and dominion, and every name that is named, not only in this age but also in that which is to come.

22 And He put all *things* under His feet, and gave Him *to be* head over all *things* to the church.

the apostle paul in reference to this event of christ siting like a king at the right of the father, says:

1 Corinthians 15:23New King James Version (NKJV)
23 But each one in his own order: Christ the first fruits, afterward those *who are* Christ's at His coming.

The church has the responsibility so that the invisible kingdom of christ may be made seen here on earth and that people may come to form part of this kingdom.This happens when the gospel is preached and people are born again.No one can see the kingdom of God unless they have been born again (john 3:3). The souls must be translocated in such a way like we have been translocated .From the darkness of satan to the kingdom of Jesus Christ.

Colossians 1:15New King James Version (NKJV)
15 He is the image of the invisible God, the firstborn over all creation.

<u>Your will be done</u> The will of God, must always be done, Jesus expresses himself in a moment of pain: saying, "Father, if it is Your will, take this cup away from Me; nevertheless not My will, but Yours, be done."

Romans 12:2New King James Version (NKJV)
2 And do not be conformed to this world, but be transformed by the renewing of your mind, that you may prove what *is* that good and acceptable and perfect will of God.

Likewise, every leader must seek what is the perfect and pleasing will of God for each one of his plans or goals and not let us be dragged by what others are doing, if the others are bankrupt then soon we will be dragged by those same currents.

Matthew 7:21New King James Version (NKJV)
21 "Not everyone who says to Me, 'Lord, Lord,' shall enter the kingdom of heaven, but he who does the will of My Father in heaven.

The most effective way so that you can know the will of God is by his word and by living works of his commandments.

This teaches us that every good leader should not just always pray, but to seek the will of God, the well-informed leader is always worth for two.

The Bible is full of instructions about how we should lead our lives. It is important to hear the Word but much more important is to be doers of the Word.

James 1:22New King James Version (NKJV)
22 But be doers of the word, and not hearers only, deceiving yourselves.

That is the will of God. That we May be doers of the Word. We can not pray, "Thy will be done" if we are not living in that will. There is no mystery in this. The will of God will be done on earth as people like you and me are willing to obey and not make cheap excuses to why they cant do this or that.

John 14:21New King James Version (NKJV)
21 He who has My commandments and keeps them, it is he who loves Me. And he who loves Me will be loved by My Father, and I will love him and manifest Myself to him."

On earth as in Heaven

God's will is perfect, and we must learn that his plans are plans of good and not evil for us, so we accept his will, whatever it is, for all works for good to those who Love him
(Jeremiah 29:11,Romans8:28)

Matthew 16:19New King James Version (NKJV)

19 And I will give you the keys of the kingdom of heaven, and whatever you bind on earth will be bound in heaven, and whatever you loose on earth will be loosed in heaven."

God teaches his children the right we have, both in heaven and on earth, for our father says that if we have the key of prayer we can do mighty things on earth because they will be unleashed in heaven, so that they descend into the Earth.

Give us this day our daily bread

God teaches us that He is the Provider and that he knows our needs, and we as his children can ask for our needs, without doubting, or strive because in God we don't lack anything, but he says ask and it will be given to you.

Luke 11:9New King James Version (NKJV)
9 "So I say to you, ask, and it will be given to you; seek, and you will find; knock, and it will be opened to you.

Matthew 6:26New King James Version (NKJV)
26 Look at the birds of the air, for they neither sow nor reap nor gather into barns; yet your heavenly Father feeds them. Are you not of more value than they?

The apostle paul says

Philippians 4:19New King James Version (NKJV)
19 And my God shall supply all your need according to His riches in glory by Christ Jesus.

The Leader must trust in God. He is our Provider. He is aware of everything we need and can, and wants to provide for us. The relationship with God must be daily, if we want to see the blessing of God daily. Perhaps you will never become a millionaire but if you are faithful to God and are obedient, and just do his will, then you can say as the psalmist said:

Psalm 37:25New King James Version (NKJV)
I have been young, and *now* am old; Yet I have not seen the righteous forsaken, Nor his descendants begging bread.

Forgive us our debts as we forgive our debtors

This portion of the prayer is extremely important for his disciples, leaders etc.God does not forgive those who do not forgive.How many times have we said God forgive us, but we have not been able to forgive our fellow man, and it is here where much leadership fails.From the treasure of the heart speaks the mouth, and many leaders are bitter because of unforgiveness, Bitterness turns into a hate tree.

Hebrews 12:15New King James Version (NKJV)
15 looking carefully lest anyone fall short of the grace of God; lest any root of bitterness springing up cause trouble, and by this many become defiled;

There are many leaders who, sooner or later, pollute the environment of their work zone because of unforgiveness.

We find followers or disciples who can not see the authority image in a leader, or that lack submission to a spiritual Father or mentor for the Simple reason he was abused by his Father, or hurt by some leader in his past and this leads him against all that is authority. But what we have to understand is that, "How can we ask God's forgiveness?" If we can not forgive those who offend us.

To forgive is to forget. Someone said forgetting is impossible when someone hurts you, but it will not be impossible with the help of God, because God forgives us and promises never to remember your sins,you may not completely forget, but at least when you remember you will not feel that Attachment to the past of resentment, and that is spiritual health.

When you forgive it does not mean that the one who hurt you is right or has had a right to hurt you, no, absolutely not, but forgiving means, if God forgave me why cant i forgive. Sometimes our debt was bigger than the one that was done to us. The main purpose of forgiving is that you are free so that nothing is binding you to a ghost of the past or a memory .Be free today and forgive, so that God will always forgive you.

And do not lead us in temptation but deliver us from evil

Many misunderstand, but it is clear that God never tempts, but allows temptation on the part of Satan, because of sin, but God will never give a test that has no way out. but what he wants is for us to pray, to not let ourselves be carried away by the temptations of the wicked, but to be free to withstand all temptation, the Bible says:

James 4:7New King James Version (NKJV)

7 Therefore submit to God. Resist the devil and he will flee from you.

James 1:13New King James Version (NKJV)
13 Let no one say when he is tempted, "I am tempted by God"; for God cannot be tempted by evil, nor does He Himself tempt anyone.

Jesus said in: John 17:15New King James Version (NKJV)
15 I do not pray that You should take them out of the world, but that You should keep them from the evil one.

I believe that there are two ways in which Satan can touch us, First, only with God's permission, job and peter are examples of this. secondly if we give him permission.

Ephesians 4:27New King James Version (NKJV)
27 nor give place to the devil.

Hebrews 4:15New King James Version (NKJV)
15 For we do not have a High Priest who cannot sympathize with our weaknesses, but was in all *points* tempted as *we are, yet* without sin.

For Yours is the kingdom and the power and the glory forever(Matthew6:13)

This is a declaration of Adoration, and supreme Praise to a King, which teaches us that we must always declare His greatness, so that our enemy may flee, for if there is anything that our adversary does not like, is this Eternal declaration, and at the same time Prophetic declaration, for declaring this we strip our enemy of any argument that he may have against the citizens of the Kingdom of God.

We end with a powerful statement, which Satan does not like, The Kingdom speaks of the territory of God, which is established here and now in our lives, according to the Power, the **Dunamis** from greek,the power of God is operating in his children of light, to proclaim the Gospel to every creature. Lastly the glory, which solely pertains to God, through out all centuries amen, and no one else but God.

Isaiah 6:3New King James Version (NKJV)
3 And one cried to another and said:

"Holy, holy, holy *is* the Lord of hosts; The whole earth *is* full of His glory!"

Revelation 19:6New King James Version (NKJV)
6 And I heard, as it were, the voice of a great multitude, as the sound of many waters and as the sound of mighty thunderings, saying, "Alleluia! For the[a] Lord God Omnipotent reigns!

CHAPTER 7
V.I.R.T.U.E.

First I want you to understand what the word virtue means. Virtue is integrity and moral excellence, power and strength, chastity, purity. It is also a quality that allows the person who owns it, to help him in the most difficult situations to change them in his favor. The virtuous is the one who is on their way to being wise, because he knows how to reach his goals without treading on others goals. He puts others on his side and leads them to reach a different goal. The virtuous is the one who "knows how to row against the current".

Also, a virtuous person is one who knows how to overcome any problem that is coming. He is a person who has many qualities and puts them into practice on a daily basis. The person who wants to be virtuous strives to acquire that good habit that makes a man capable to fulfill whats good.

Virtues are considered positive qualities, and are opposed to vices. Virtues are the good and sensitive qualities of the human being.

Exodus 18:14-26New King James Version (NKJV)
14 So when Moses' father-in-law saw all that he did for the people, he said, "What *is* this thing that you are doing for the people? Why do you alone sit, and all the people stand before you from morning until evening?"**15** And Moses said to his father-in-law, "Because the people come to me to inquire of God. **16** When they have a difficulty, they come to me, and I judge between one and another; and I make known the statutes of God and His laws."**17** So Moses' father-in-law said to him, "The thing that you do *is* not good. **18** Both you and these people who *are* with you will surely

wear yourselves out. For this thing *is* too much for you; you are not able to perform it by yourself. **19** Listen now to my voice; I will give you counsel, and God will be with you: Stand before God for the people, so that you may bring the difficulties to God. **20** And you shall teach them the statutes and the laws, and show them the way in which they must walk and the work they must do. **21** Moreover you shall select from all the people able men, such as fear God, men of truth, hating covetousness; and place *such* over them *to be* rulers of thousands, rulers of hundreds, rulers of fifties, and rulers of tens. **22** And let them judge the people at all times. Then it will be *that* every great matter they shall bring to you, but every small matter they themselves shall judge. So it will be easier for you, for they will bear *the burden* with you. **23** If you do this thing, and God *so* commands you, then you will be able to endure, and all this people will also go to their place in peace."**24** So Moses heeded the voice of his father-in-law and did all that he had said. **25** And Moses chose able men out of all Israel, and made them heads over the people: rulers of thousands, rulers of hundreds, rulers of fifties, and rulers of tens. **26** So they judged the people at all times; the hard cases they brought to Moses, but they judged every small case themselves.

This was good for Moses. He could focus on the most important things and would not be overwhelmed and stressed by many small tasks.

This was good for the leaders Moses chose. They gave to capable men a real responsibility, and had the opportunity to serve the people of God in a meaningful way to extend the work of God.

This was good for the congregation. Moses prayed and taught them, and they were able to resolve more matters for themselves. When they needed to resolve an issue, they received better attention from the delegate leaders than Moses himself. "It's better to put a hundred men to work than to do the work of a hundred men." (D.L. Moody)

Acronym of the word
V.I.R.T.U.R.E.

.**V**ision

.**I**ntegrity

.**R**esponsibility

.**T**estify

.**U**nity

.**E**ntrust

Vision

Vision is the goal that you want to reach. Without vision there is no direction. Not having vision is like getting into a taxi and not giving him an address, just going for a ride without knowing where it leads to. It is like boarding a ship without a map or GPS on the high seas, or like a plane without coordinates. My question is: Would you get on a car to take you to your destination knowing that the car has no steering wheel?

Vision is the image of the future that we want to see for the Organization or ministry. That is why vision gives you direction, and security. The best example of a lack of vision is when you get in an automobile and you are on a road where the weather is rainy and foggy, and your vision becomes really short and you can not go faster, you feel insecure and those who go with you will feel the same way.

Habakkuk 2: 2-4 (New King James Version)
2 Then the Lord answered me and said: "Write the vision And make *it* plain on tablets, That he may run who reads it.

3 For the vision *is* yet for an appointed time; But at the end it will speak, and it will not lie. Though it tarries, wait for it; Because it will surely come, It will not tarry.

4 "Behold the proud, His soul is not upright in him; But the just shall live by his faith.

Write the vision of the goals you want to accomplish, and if the vision is clear, and everyone can read it, they will feel safe and with direction. The team's strength will be used to push towards the same direction and this will give you growth and acceleration and speed to extend the ministry.

When there is no vision everyone wants to push the cart toward different directions, some don't even want to get help push it, but when everyone reads the vision of where we want to get, there will be better results in the effort that everyone puts. That is why every leader must and always needs to have a vision and present it to his team.

Integrity

Integrity is translated as honored, honest, respect for others, direct, appropriate, responsible, emotional control, respect for self, punctuality, loyalty, neat, disciplined, congruence and firmness in their actions. In general, it is someone you can trust. Integrity is to return to the path of our truth, to do what is right, for the right reasons, in the right way.

From the ethical point of view, it would be the way to be managed coherently with personal values and shared with the community to which it belongs.

It is our ability to make and fulfill commitments to ourselves, to do what we say. His discipline comes from within; it is a function of their independent will. You are a disciple, a follower of your ingrained own values, and you have the will and the integrity to subordinate to those values, your feelings, your impulses and your state of mind (Stephen Covey: "Seven habits of effective people").

The Hebrew terms related to the word "integrity" come from a root meaning "intact," "without blemish or defect." And one of these Hebrew terms is used to refer to the animals that were offered to Jehovah.So that he would accept them, they had to be healthy and without defects or Jehovah would condemn energetically those who disobeyed that rule and offered animals lame, sick, and blind. (Read Leviticus 22:19, 20 and Malachi 1:6-8).

We read that the symbolism of the sacrifice in the old covenant was that the Messiah would come and give Himself to be the perfect sacrifice to pay our transgressions and sins. We really have the most powerful supernatural example recorded on earth, an integral man like Jesus Christ came about 2000 years ago and through that leader, today, we can all come and receive the mighty gift of eternity.

Responsibility

It is a capacity that every leader must have, it is to be able to recognize the consequences of our actions or decision, If a leader does not have this he will never be able to improve as a person.Always leaving things started and it will be very easy to abandon difficult projects or leave his team behind or unattended and this will be dangerous for the leadership.

Responsibility is a value that is in the consciousness of a person, which allows him to reflect, manage, guide and value the consequences of his actions, always on the moral plane.

The responsible person is one who acts consciously being the direct cause of an event that occurred. He is responding to respond for something or someone. It is also someone who fulfills his obligations or that puts care and attention in what he does or decides.

Romans 14:12New King James Version (NKJV)

12 So then each of us shall give account of himself to God.

1 Corinthians 5:10New King James Version (NKJV)

10 Yet *I* certainly *did* not *mean* with the sexually immoral people of this world, or with the covetous, or extortioners, or idolaters, since then you would need to go out of the world.

Matthew 12:36New King James Version (NKJV)

36 But I say to you that for every idle word men may speak, they will give account of it in the day of judgment.

The Leader is responsible in all aspects of his life, it is very painful to see leaders who are vainly expressing "I am like that " so " What ?, I think whats most embarrassing is calling the attention to an irresponsible person, because when they are responsible and you tell them their Mistakes they accept you with annoyance and grief, but accept it and makes changes. But call your attention to an irresponsible person and it will be appalling.

Testify

Of all the possible origins of the word testify, the one that seems more reliable and is supported by more experts is the one that indicates that it derives from the word witness, and this one in turn comes from the old Iberian word "Testiguar", derived from Latin "Testificare". "Testificare" is composed of "testis" (witness) and "Facere" (to do).

A true ambassador is a witness of what he represents, the true witness is saying that not only is someone who has knowledge of something, but lives what he preaches.

To testify is to announce something proven, that is how every company, every product, or every ministry will have acceptance and a healthy growth. Everything that is recommended by a testimony means that it is reliable, and every consumer will feel safe and confident that he may invest time and money,and even their daily living.

It is sad to know that there are very few Christians who testify about their faith, or about their church, or of their relationship with brothers in the faith, etc ... And the reason is because they have forgotten that the best way to evangelize someone is with his own testimony, this is why Jesus Christ had thousands of followers, because they all testified about Him.

Witnessing is the true and most honest publicity you can use to promote the gospel, church, ministry, bible study.

V.I.R.T.U.E. -page ??

The biggest companies have found the key to selling their products and have greater reach through consumers testimony. This is why today it is possible to monitor an image on screen, or through social media and the reason is because they are interested in what people think of their products.

(Read Acts 1: 8) "and you shall be witnesses to Me ... and to the end of the earth."

Unity

A definition for unity can be this: Property that has things that can not be fragmented or divided without being altered or destroyed. One of the most difficult things is to make changes, or to set new goals, or give a new direction to a project. The truth is that it takes the unity of an entire team to have an impact on a transformation. When a group of employees form a union to express some dissatisfaction and bring change to a company, the most effective way is for all workers to join and sign the contract, until including the supervisors.

One of our greatest enemies in our leadership is precisely the division or disunion of the group. Personally I have realized that when our enemy, the devil, sees that he has no open doors to enter, he will always seek his last and effective weapon, and that is the disunion of a team. I have seen this in orchestras, chorus groups, sports teams, marriages, churches, companies, etc ...

There is a very famous saying that says: "The united people will never be defeated" and it really is so.

Friends and brothers united together we are stronger. United to God and to our family we will be very strong Christians.

That is why a person who does not know or does not like to work in unity will never be able to reach new levels in all senses of his life, be it spiritual, material, or emotional, etc...

(John 17:21-22 NKJV)
"**21** that they all may be one, as You, Father, are in Me, and I in You; that they also may be one in Us, that the world may believe that You sent Me. **22** And the glory which You gave Me I have given them, that they may be one just as We are one."

Entrust

The meaning of entrust is to give a power, a role, or responsibility to another person, to exercise in place.

This is when the leader really is multiplied, that is, he will never stop fructifying what he sowed. When you delegate, it means something very important, this is that you did the job of training or teaching someone and now you have the confidence to give that person a responsibility of yours, and doing that gives you the time for you as a leader to administer yourself better in other areas. A simple but important example is:

Many times leaders do not want to give keys to anyone of the premises or the church, and you always find a pressured leader. Since there are times that obstacles may arise to open up a premises. However, if someone else has the key then I think it will be easier to solve the problem, because the more people that are able to take on that responsibility there will be more options to solve problems.

Entrusting will give you rest and at the same time it will give you more production because if the leader can lead less tired or pressured he can lead his team with more diligence and wisdom. A tired leader is the worst there can be in a team, It is like when you travel by car and 4 people know how to drive but the owner of the car never lets others drive, if the trip is more than 8 hours you will have a dangerous driver, risking the lives of others. However, if you have the confidence to entrust shifts to the wheel, everyone can move forward and rest at the same time.

Entrusting is to secure the future of any ministry. Jesus Christ entrusted the work to his Church, to proclaim salvation and eternal life, to this day the Church is the most powerful Spiritual Organism on earth.

Entrusting is assuring that although you are no longer there some one else will do it.

Read Matthew 18-20

Mark 16:15-18New King James Version (NKJV)

15 And He said to them, "Go into all the world and preach the gospel to every creature. **16** He who believes and is baptized will be saved; but he who does not believe will be condemned.**17** And these signs will follow those who believe: In My name they will cast out demons; they will speak with new tongues;**18** they will take up serpents; and if they drink anything deadly, it will by no means hurt them; they will lay hands on the sick, and they will recover."

CHAPTER 8

THE VALUE OF ONE

I want to explain this title. I will begin with The Value. There is a great importance in what takes value in your life, because if your thought is equal to the one who does not value life, believe me that you will end badly. It will be no good to you to win or have success in your life as a leader. Sooner or later you will end up self-destructing and dragging yourself down to a level in which you loose respect for others and you become an egocentric leader, or even come to despise your work team, or worse you can come to despise what God has already given you personally.

Some definitions of the word value are quality, virtue, or utility that make something or someone appreciated; Importance of a thing, action, word or phrase, or in plural values. Ideological or moral principles are guided by a society and can also mean the value of bravery, or quality of bravery.

By these definitions it takes a lot of courage for a leader to know how to value himself, but also to know how to value others, because a supernatural leader inspires others to bring out the best in them, but he will never be able to achieve it, if he does not recognize his own value and the value of others. This is where having value for others come in.

For a level of teamwork, in an organization or ministry. I like what Juan Carlos Jiménez wrote in his book The Value of Values:

Values are principles that allow us to guide our behavior as a function to realize ourselves as people. They are fundamental beliefs that help us to prefer, appreciate and choose things from others, or behavior instead of another. They are also a source of satisfaction and fulfillment.

They provide a guideline for formulating goals and purposes, personal or collective. They reflect our most important interests, feelings, and convictions.

Values refer to human needs and represent ideals, dreams and aspirations, with an independent importance of the circumstances. For example, even if we are unjust, justice still has value. The same applies to the well-being or happiness.

The values fend for themselves. They are important for what they are, what they mean, and what they represent, not what they are about.

Values, attitudes, and behaviors are closely related. When we speak of attitude we refer to the willingness to act at any time, in accordance with our beliefs, feelings and values.

Values are translated into thoughts, concepts or ideas, but what we most appreciate is behavior, what people do. A valuable person is someone who lives by the values in which he believes. She is worth what her values are worth and the way she lives it.

But values are also the basis for community and relating to other people. They allow us to regulate our behavior for collective well-being and harmonious coexistence.

Perhaps for this reason we have the tendency to relate them according to rules and norms of behavior, but in reality they are decisions. This is to say that we decide to act one way and not another based on what is important to us as value. We decide to believe in that and to appreciate it in a special way.

When we reach an organization with already defined values, we implicitly assume accepting and putting them into practice. It is what other members of the organization expect from us.

In an organization values are the framework of the behavior that its members must have, and depend on the nature of the organization (its reason for being), the purpose for which it was created (its objectives), and their projection into the future (their vision). In order to do this, they should inspire the attitudes and actions necessary to achieve their objectives.

In other words, organizational values should be reflected especially in the details of what most of the members of the organization do daily, rather than in their general statements. If this does not happen the organization must review how to work its values. (Juan Carlos Jiménez)

Romans 12:3New King James Version (NKJV)
3 For I say, through the grace given to me, to everyone who is among you, not to think of himself more highly than he ought to think, but to think soberly, as God has dealt to each one a measure of faith.

Your investment will always be in what you value. If you believe that you have something that God already gave and you value it, then you can invest your time, your strength and your money and so you will be successful. But how many times does what happened to me, at the age of 16, occur. When I would say "God can use that boy or that lady or that other person but me". But one day God confronted me, and he spoke to me through a conference lecturer, and looking me in the eyes and without knowing me, said to me, "You say God is Great and Almighty, but you do not believe that I can use you to make a difference." The truth is I had a thought like that, until I valued what God had given me since I was a boy,and that was Music, which i had in low esteem due to negative opinions towards my talent. but believe me that it was necessary for me to learn to value my talent before it could be unleashed and believe that God could use me. And this is where the value of One comes in.

Someone once said one is like none, but everyone takes this phrase wrong because they take it as the figure of one. It was nothing or almost nothing or none, when what is really being said is that One has the value and mathematically speaking one is the first number with value,and can make the difference between zero or one, between something or nothing. If you lack a cent you will have 99 cents but if you have a cent more you will complete 1 dollar. Games are won by 1 second. By 1 vote elections are won. By one point World Cups and Olympics are won. Through one man we lost a lot in the world, but by one man we won the whole universe. Through the Value of One we will do great things.

As an interesting detail the number zero did not exist nor was used in the Hebrew numbers, nor Greek nor Roman, until the fifteenth century. It was introduced completely in Europe and the West and we gave it full use in our numbers, influenced by the Arabs, who took from Indian culture the number zero. And although it is believed that the Mayans and the Toltecs used the zero, it was not until the fifteenth century when it was actually implemented in our modern culture and has taken a great place in Algebra and in the language of computers. In reality, mathematically speaking zero has no numerical value until after it has a number 1 to its left, in example the number 10. The zero to the left has no value, and I believe that there are many who feel like zero to the left of a number 1, but here I want to inspire you by means of parable.

PARABLE OF THE TALENTS

Matthew 25:14-30New King James Version (NKJV)
14 "For the kingdom of heaven is like a man traveling to a far country, who called his own servants and delivered his goods to them. 15 And to one he gave five talents, to another two, and to another one, to each according to his own ability; and immediately he went on a journey. 16 Then he who had received the five talents went and traded with them, and made another five talents. 17 And likewise he who had received two gained two more also. 18 But he who had received one went and dug in the ground, and hid his lord's money. 19 After a long time the lord of those servants came and settled accounts with them.

20 "So he who had received five talents came and brought five other talents, saying, 'Lord, you delivered to me five talents; look, I have gained five more talents besides them.' 21 His lord said to him, 'Well done, good and faithful servant; you were faithful over a few things, I will make you ruler over many things. Enter into the joy of your lord.' 22 He also who had received two talents came and said, 'Lord, you delivered to me two talents; look, I have gained two more talents besides them.' 23 His lord said to him, 'Well done, good and faithful servant; you have been faithful over a few things, I will make you ruler over many things. Enter into the joy of your lord.'

24 "Then he who had received the one talent came and said, 'Lord, I knew you to be a hard man, reaping where you have not sown, and gathering

where you have not scattered seed. 25 And I was afraid, and went and hid your talent in the ground. Look, there you have what is yours.'

26 "But his lord answered and said to him, 'You wicked and lazy servant, you knew that I reap where I have not sown, and gather where I have not scattered seed. 27 So you ought to have deposited my money with the bankers, and at my coming I would have received back my own with interest. 28 Therefore take the talent from him, and give it to him who has ten talents.

29 'For to everyone who has, more will be given, and he will have abundance; but from him who does not have, even what he has will be taken away. 30 And cast the unprofitable servant into the outer darkness. There will be weeping and gnashing of teeth.'

The term parable means comparison, likeness. Jesus used allegories and metaphors to teach. There is something very exclusive of the biblical parables that are used to explain the kingdom of heaven through the things of this world that represent or symbolize the spiritual ones.

The parable begins with the phrase: The Kingdom of Heaven "is Like" here we know that it symbolizes something, it is like a man going away, that called his servants and he delivered them his goods. The part that strikes me most is not that he gave them his goods, but that he gave them according to each ones capacity. One he gave 5 talents, another 2, and another one, but to each according to his ability.

Here begins a very important teaching in leadership and that is that we must know the capacity of each person, iouch! The Master is getting us into a very delicate terrain, especially in the Churches. But this doesn't just happen in the churches, but also in sports teams, in companies, etc.

How often do you come to a congregation where the one who is directing the worship is not able to lead a whole group to sing in the right key? or the correct rhythm, and does not even feel the calling to do what he is doing. Or for example the ushers at the doors of the church have a sad face or don't give a cordial greeting to the guests.From those that receive at the doors to those that teach classes and to the ones that participate in dramas at church. it is sad to see the church being managed by those that are favored, or because they voted as if it were a political post, or because this one is "spiritual" or because there is no other way.

Truly we need to let the holy spirit of God raise up supernatural leaders, who are skilled and filled with the holy spirit.

Acts 6:3New King James Version (NKJV)
3 Therefore, brethren, seek out from among you seven men of *good* reputation, full of the Holy Spirit and wisdom, whom we may appoint over this business;

I would like to make a parenthesis here, we understand that when someone starts we work with what we have.But the problem lies that there are occasions were years pass and no one becomes capacitated to truly fulfill with virtue the privileges that are assigned to them.Or no one strives to really appreciate and value what they have been given. The Bible says in 1 Samuel 16 that David knows how to play, and he is brave and vigorous and a man of war, prudent in his words, and beautiful, and Jehovah is with him. WOW! what a way to describe this young man.There was a reason why he put him to sing for the King. The teacher began with 12 disciples, who when they started we notice their defects and mistakes, like the famous Peter, which Jesus himself said to him away from me satan. Matthew 16:23New King James Version (NKJV)
23 But He turned and said to Peter, "Get behind Me, Satan! You are an offense to Me, for you are not mindful of the things of God, but the things of men."

Peter had plans outside of the Master's vision but he was corrected. What I like about Peter is that he was a disciple who never settled, and who fought until he became a great leader among the apostles.

Jesus saw something in Peter that despite his mistakes, and even after denying him 3 times. Jesus restored him and encouraged him to be a great shepherd of his sheep. We could say that Peter and the apostles had 3 and a half years of process to become great men of God, really prepared for the great commission.

Peter was only one of the examples, each disciple had his faults, but the Master put each one in his place according to their capacity.

We can confirm it in the Apostle Paul that although he did not walk 3 and a half years with Jesus when he was on earth, we know that he succeeded in being one of the most used apostles who wrote more than everyone else in the New Testament.

His preparation for the service took about ten years, more or less. First in Damascus, Acts 9:20, 21; In Arabia, Galatians 1:17; In Damascus again, Acts 9: 22-25; A visit to Jerusalem, 9: 26-30, Galatians 1:18; In his native city, Tarsus, Acts 9:30, 11:25; And in Antioch with Barnabas and the local church, 11:25, 26.

Paul was born in Tarsus, the Greek capital of Southeast Asia, in a non insignificant city of Cilicia. "Near Athens and Alexandria, Tarsus was a universal center, and its students would be gathered from the East and West.He was a Benjamite with the same name as the first king of Israel.Paul knew the trade of fabricating tents from goat hair. He was also educated in a liberal and Greek environment, but received his theological education at the feet of Gamaliel in Jerusalem.Paul became a strict Pharisee, characterized by intolerance and fanaticism. It is uncertain whether or not he was a member of the Sanhedrin, the parliament of the jewish. This period of his life occupied about thirty-five years, almost half of his life.

Again we can see a man truly prepared but at the same time full of the power of the Holy Spirit. A great leader with the supernatural of God in his life.Paul was a man with knowledge and Manifestation, Law and grace, Circumcision and Crucifixion, a man bearing the marks of his Master in his body and In his spirit, a vertical and horizontal life, with power and word, full of prayer and action, theology and practice.

A man who after his conversion to Christ, despite his preparation and his personal calling directly from the Master, waits about a 10-year process period to fully embrace his ministry.

Something I want to make clear, the leadership in your life begins today, someone ones said 'never leave for tomorrow what you can do today', and it is very true, there are people who are always preparing and never do anything for the works of the lord, or for their lives or for their families, or even for themselves.They are always in the process, maybe it sounds funny but there are people who have been Christians for years, and they speak obscene words or cuss word slips out of their tongues and the excuse is that they are living a Process, "God is doing his work in me".Living the process and God working in us is true, but please! you've been on the same page for ten years. I think it is time to really value what we have in our hands and in our reach. Therefore It is time to give the best of us every single day.

God will ask you like he did Moses "WHAT IS THAT YOU HAVE IN YOUR HANDS"? And Moses said a rod, (Exodus 4: 2) God will tell you the same: USE IT.

Many times what you have in your hands may not be much, but here is where the key to one's worth is; In the parable we see three Servants to whom different amounts are given, to one 5 talents was given, to another 2 talents, and to another 1 talent, here the word to "**another**" reminds me of a key scripture that is in the book of 1Corinthians, chapter 12, Where these same words appear.Each one were given gifts or abilities and it says " one of faith, and another to speak tongues, and another utterance of knowledge, etc."

In this parabola they mention a measure of value, Just how the Talent is.

to understand this, heres an example, if a denarius is equivalent to 4 grams of silver, then one talent was worth 6,000 denarius. A Jewish day laborer earned a denarius in a whole day's work (Matthew 20: 2) If a laborer wanted to gain only one talent, he would have to work 6,000 days or 20 years!

If we do the correct calculations, we can understand that the servant who received 5 talents actually received a salary of 100 years, the one who received 2 talents received the equivalence of a salary of 40 years, And the one who received only 1 talent was receiving the salary of 20 years of work.

We can see that the servant that was given one was given something, but he did not know how to value it. In order to grow something you need to value it and that is why I want to share with you this rule of 5 things that we must consider for growth, I call it the **5 attitudes to increase.**

 # 1 You have to see what God sees. God has a perfect plan, but we often can not see it, do not look at the quantity, circumstances, obstacles, or how great of a mountain, but rather look at the Father and throw yourself in his arms because he knows what you are capable of achieving.

Jeremiah 29:11New King James Version (NKJV)
For I know the thoughts that I think toward you, says the Lord, thoughts of peace and not of evil, to give you a future and a hope.

Isaiah 55:8-9New King James Version (NKJV)
"For My thoughts *are* not your thoughts, Nor *are* your ways My ways," says the Lord.

"For *as* the heavens are higher than the earth, So are My ways higher than your ways, And My thoughts than your thoughts.

For if you can achieve to see yourself as God sees you, and discover the true purpose for which you exist, you will put all your investment in it and then begin to multiply and increase your success.

 # 2 Discerning in you, is to invest in what is safe. If you ignore your potential, you will be in danger of never investing in what can give you the best results, knowing that you have a talent, a gift, an ability to do something, and the best part is you are good at it and you know it because you enjoy it and you do it better than anyone else.

If you can not see the talent in you, you will never take care of it, or protect it, nor will you make it prosper, much less invest in it. Ephesians 4: 8 says it very clearly, our master gave gifts to men, If there is something you must see is that you have something within you and you are not here by coincidence.

 # 3 Do not compare with your godfathers. We have to stop looking at the grass in front of us, because the neighbor's grass will always look greener from your house, because it is almost certain that when you go to your neighbor's house and look at your house you will realize that your grass does not look as bad as you thought; This is just an anecdote but it is a reality.We have to stop seeing what others have, how they have it and if they have more than us, it's time to act.

Stop seeing the talents and gifts of others because if not you will always be following others for their talents and that will hinder you to focus on yours, and you will never recognize yours, you have identity. if it is one gift, ok good, perfect, your capacity is one, and you know that you will be the best one that exists.

Never feel less to have less, because it is not what you have what gives you value, but what has you, or keeps you,and it is not what you hold, but what you give, what makes you virtuous.If you achieve to reproduce what you have, you will always have something to give,making you a successful person.

Romans 12: 3 teaches us to never have a wrong concept of ourselves, neither too high nor too low, we must always be blessed, grateful and positive.

 # 4 Grateful and content but never compliant and slow. Everyone has been given, but some were given more than others, always live grateful for what you were given, because gratitude is the key to fullness.

Thank you God for this 1 talent that has been given to me, and with that one I will be the best to multiply it and someday be of 2 talents, and if I can reach 5 talents glory to God.Thank you God for the 1 talent because today I know that I have the best, because if you had not given me that 1 talent i might of never came out of my conformity and i might of never had the opportunity to be a part of the history of humanity.

Philippians 4:11-13New King James Version (NKJV)
11 Not that I speak in regard to need, for I have learned in whatever state I am, to be content: **12** I know how to be abased, and I know how to abound. Everywhere and in all things I have learned both to be full and to be hungry, both to abound and to suffer need. **13** I can do all things through Christ[a] who strengthens me.

Carnality destroys creativity, jealousy is deadly, that is why you never get infected by those who speak to you in the ear and tell you "why did they give you less". you just say to them "they gave me"and that's all I know and I'm going to be thankful, And I will not settle until one day i deserve another level, so that way i may remain faithful servant. Therefore I am happy but I will not be slow, but the day to grow is today, I will work, and work,and I know that I will succeed, hasten and accelerate my steps oh God to do what I heard yesterday.

#5 Excellence in your potential.

Be excellent at your own level. We must always do our best.There are times when the meaning of the word excellence in leadership is confused. We always hear in many leaders if I had this or that, then it could be excellent, always referring to the economic potential and I think that's completely loosing focus, I'll explain: Excelence means to give the maximum recognition to a person, thing or situation; If we really want to do something for God, or for our company, home or family, we must do it with excellence.Truly recognizing the value of what we are doing, example: If I am going to prepare a conference or meeting, everything should be clean, in place, and ready to be used, that's excellence. There are times we thought if we had giant screens, a giant place, and a giant pulpit then it would be excellence, and that's where we are wrong, we can be small places but be a place of excellence, starting with the leadership, well dressed, clean,presentable,and a place with good music, good word and a supernatural atmosphere full of the presence of God. I can assure you that people will say what an excellent place that is.

Someone ones said "the suit does not make the monk but identifies him" and the saying is so true.

I want to finish this chapter by giving these last tips that we can learn from this beautiful parable of the talents.The parable teaches that the master gave them according to their ability and did not give them because of his preference. God will give you according to your ability, God does not expect that a person of 2 talents works to the capacity of a person of 5 talents, but God does wants you to work on your level of ability or level of Faith as the Bible says:

Romans 12:3New King James Version (NKJV)
3 For I say, through the grace given to me, to everyone who is among you, not to think *of himself* more highly than he ought to think, but to think soberly, as God <u>has dealt to each one a measure of faith.</u>

Thanks to God for this opportunity that he has gave me to share with you dear reader, this book which i titled **Supernatural Leadership**, I will soon present another book of leadership and other works that God has allowed me to write. Thank you and I ask for your prayer so that God may finish his purpose in me.

CONCLUSION

God designed you with a purpose, and you are not a product of chance. Dear reader, never give up, do the works that God has commanded you to do. A sign is that what troubles you and does not let you sleep needs you, and you are the one who can make the difference. Do not miss this beautiful and valuable opportunity God gives you of existence, no one can tell you who you are or what you are, only you and God can define that. Remember that every work take time, be patient, since you can learn from creation, see that when God wants an oak tree or a large tree it takes years for growing, but when a fungus forms it is done overnight. Give the best of yourself every day, as if it were the last day of your life, and remember that giving is better than receiving. Love God and your neighbor, forgive all those who offend you and you will succeed in everything you do, because without true love you will never achieve the supernatural, be responsible for your actions and Allow God to be your guide, God needs men and women who are an example. But do not forget that you need him more, because without him we are nothing, you can be the leader with many material things, but if you do not have God, I do not care how much wealth you have, without God we are lost. A leader without God will never go from this earth to eternity, so prepare and seek the kingdom of God and his justice. Make history where you are and be part of a generation of supernatural leaders that God has prepared for this time.

Philippians 4: 11-13 NIV
11 Not that I speak in regard to need, for I have learned in whatever state I am, to be content: **12** I know how to be abased, and I know how to abound. Everywhere and in all things I have learned both to be full and to be hungry, both to abound and to suffer need. **13** I can do all things through Christ who strengthens me.

Printed in the United States
By Bookmasters